Quick
&Easy

The
Well-Behaved
Family Dog

Diane Morgan

*Quick & Easy® The Well-Behaved
Family Dog*

Project Team
Editor: Adam Taliercio
Copy Editor: Stephanie Fornino
Indexer: Ann W. Truesdale
Cover and interior design: Angela Stanford

T.F.H. Publications
President/CEO: Glen S. Axelrod
Executive Vice President: Mark E. Johnson
Publisher: Christopher T. Reggio
Production Manager: Kathy Bontz

T.F.H. Publications, Inc.
One TFH Plaza
Third and Union Avenues
Neptune City, NJ 07753

07 08 09 10 11 1 3 5 7 9 8 6 4 2
Printed and bound in China
Library of Congress Cataloging-in-Publication Data
Morgan, Diane, 1947-
  Quick & easy the well-behaved family dog : step-by-step techniques for parenting a happy
dog / Diane Morgan.
     p. cm.
  Includes index.
  ISBN 978-0-7938-1005-5 (alk. paper)
 1. Dogs--Training. I. Title. II. Title: Quick and easy the well-behaved family dog.

SF431.M8225 2007
636.7'0887--dc22
                                    2007022687

The Leader in Responsible Animal Care for Over 50 Years!®
www.tfh.com

Table of Contents

Quick & Easy

Chapter 1

Training Basics

Dogs are wonderful creatures. Descended from the wild wolves of Asia, they have graciously chosen to join humanity in a partnership that covers the globe. Dogs are shepherds, guardians, bomb detectors, hunting assistants, and guides to the disabled. But most of all, they are our beloved pets and companions.

Your dog will be happier and more well adjusted if he receives training.

A Trained Dog Is a Happy Dog

Dogs' wild days are over; and that means that any dog today should be a trained dog. He may not be ready to join the circus, but he should know and obey basic commands and act in a civilized manner. A trained dog is not only more convenient to his owner but is happier, too, because he will be given more freedom and fewer restrictions.

Unfortunately, not all dogs are trained dogs. That's too bad, because an untrained, unsocialized dog is a burden to his owner, an annoyance to guests, an object of scorn to passersby, and an embarrassment to the species. Because of these things, an untrained dog is at great risk of being given up, abandoned, or even killed.

How Breed Affects Trainability

Keep your expectations realistic—not every dog is Lassie. If you want a dog for personal protection, a Cavalier King Charles Spaniel is not for you. If you want a dog who will romp effortlessly with the kids all day long, a Bulldog may disappoint you.

In the same way, some dogs are easier to train than others. Retrievers, Poodles, and German Shepherd Dogs seem eager to follow commands, while other breeds are more independent. That doesn't mean that they can't be trained, though; it just means that you have to be smart enough to figure out how to train them. Any dog can learn basic commands if you take the time and effort to teach him. When you learn to accept your dog for who he is, you'll find that he has plenty to offer.

Your Dog Is Always Learning

Training your dog is an ongoing process. As your dog matures, learns new skills, and adapts to a changing environment, he is constantly being challenged. No dog is ever finished training, just as no human is ever finished learning. This doesn't mean that training has to be an unpleasant or onerous chore. On the contrary, training your dog is the best way to bond with him, interest him, lead him, and expose him to an exciting world. (It's also fun!)

A pet dog should be able to:
- come when called
- sit and stay on command
- walk politely on a lead
- greet people calmly

Some breeds, such as the Poodle, are more eager to learn than others, but all dogs can be trained.

- stay off furniture unless invited on
- play with his own toys (while leaving your "toys" alone)
- quietly remain crated without pitching a fit
- have his nails trimmed without a fuss

Did You Know?

If you have a large or potentially dangerous dog, your failure to properly train him may result in serious physical harm to someone— and a lawsuit.

WHO'S TOP DOG IN YOUR HOUSE?

Dogs are social beings, just like their wolf ancestors. Wolves live in small, family-like packs, and so do dogs. If dogs lived solitary lives, they wouldn't need training because they wouldn't come into contact with anyone. But because dogs live in a family, they need rules about how to behave, just like the rest of us. They not only need rules—they want them. In a wild pack, every member knows who the leader is, who to look up to, and who decides where to go next. In this hierarchy system, there is *always* a top dog. In your family, *that top dog has to be you.* If you are not the leader, your dog might apply for the job. You can keep your dog from making this mistake by stepping up to your responsibility.

It's also important to remember that your dog is learning something all the time, whether you are around to train him or not. So if you have specific things you want your dog to learn, you need to be the one to teach him. Otherwise, he'll start figuring things out on his own.

TYPES OF TRAINING METHODS

There is no one perfect way to train every dog. Like people, dogs have different learning styles, and what may work well for one dog may have little effect on another. In addition, while you can get the same response from different training methods, not all methods will work equally well in helping to bond you and your dog in a loving way. For example, if you gave your dog an electric shock every time he tried to jump up on you, he would stop doing it. However, the result would be a frightened, sad, and uncertain pet. The stress of such cruel "training" would create additional behavioral problems.

The first thing to remember when preparing to train is that a dog is not a child. He is not even a human

No matter how human he may seem at times, your dog is an animal with unique needs and desires.

being. His chromosomes don't match up with ours, and you can't write him off as a dependent. If you think of your dog as a furry kid, he's bound to disappoint you. Nor is he your "best friend," despite all those sentimental sayings. He will never lend you money, take you out to dinner, or pick you up at the airport. He will listen to your problems, at least until something more interesting happens, but he doesn't really understand them and he can't give you any useful advice. However, dogs do have feelings, needs, and desires. If these are continually misunderstood, frustrated, or ignored, the outcome will be bad for both of you.

Your dog is an absolutely unique creature. His genes are the genes of the wolf, but his heart belongs to you. Don't break it.

Rather than harsh training methods that use punishment to teach, most dogs respond reasonably well to a combination of positive reinforcement, deliberate nonresponse, and occasional correction. The distinction among all these terms is not always clear and not always necessary. The goal of good training is to encourage your dog to understand and obey your

Quick Tip

One easy way to retain your "alpha dog" status is to keep your furniture for human use only. Some dominant dogs think that sleeping high up or using your special places gives them equal status to you. If this is the case with your dog, stop a potential problem before it begins and make sure that he sleeps in his own bed at ground level. Besides, who needs dog hair all over the sofa?

Quick Tip

Dogs are very quick to pick up on your mood, so never start training your pet when you are tired or angry. That won't be any fun for either of you. If you are calm and reasonable, you may be surprised at how easy your dog is to train.

wishes and discourage him from doing something dangerous.

REWARD-BASED TRAINING

Reward-based training is used to reinforce good behavior after it occurs and to encourage a dog (usually by means of a lure or bribe) into behaving the way you want during training. Rewards can come in the form of food, praise, petting, or extra play time. Once your dog learns a skill, the rewards you give him can become less frequent. Studies show that once a dog has learned a desired behavior, intermittent rewards actually achieve more ready compliance than regular, always-to-be-counted-upon rewards.

Most of the time, feeding your dog for doing what you want is still the best and quickest way to get a good result, although some dogs react just as positively to praise or play. Reward-based training is preferred whenever possible because it gets your dog to do what you want and enjoy himself at the same time.

The Benefits of Positivity

Whereas other kinds of training are merely intended to discourage bad behavior, positive training provides a dog a clue as to what he *should* do instead. Think about it this way: Let's say a bored child begins kicking the walls in his room. His mother comes in, says "Don't do that," and then leaves. Well, even if he stops kicking the walls as requested, he still doesn't have a clue what to do next, so he starts breaking the windows instead. If his mother had said "Oh, I see you feel like kicking! Let's go play kickball!" the child would have had a positive alternative to his behavior.

The Treat Should Fit the Task

The less enjoyable the activity for the dog, the greater the lure and reward have to be. For instance, Labrador Retrievers retrieve by instinct, and the behavior is so enjoyable for them that it is a reward in itself. A hound, on the other hand, is not a natural retriever and is much less likely to be interested in fetching games. This does not make a hound less intelligent than a Labrador; it just means that you have to use better lures and rewards to get him to behave like one.

DELIBERATE NONRESPONSE

This usually means simply that a dog is not rewarded in any way for doing what you don't want him to do. Because a lot of "bad" dog behavior is simply your dog's way of trying to get a little attention from you, the way to extinguish it is not to give him attention. Many unwanted behaviors will simply disappear if you don't pay attention to them. However, make no mistake: Dogs need attention. Just make sure that you only give it to your dog when he is behaving well. If you always ignore your dog, deliberate nonresponse won't have any effect on him.

Dogs respond best to positive reinforcement in the form of treats, praise, or even play.

CORRECTION

Correction can range from a stern "No!" to a sharp tug on the collar. While the line between correction and punishment can be blurry, there is a distinction. Usually "correction" refers to an action that is mild, quick, and instantaneous. It can be a word, a look, or a clap of the hands. If done right, a verbal correction or a hard look may be all that your dog ever needs; it is the human version of a dog's growl. At the least it gets his attention and is often very effective.

The biggest mistake people make when correcting their dog is starting too soon or too late, in which case the correction is actually counterproductive. Timing is everything in training.

PUNISHMENT

Punishment is more severe and lasts longer than correction, and it doesn't work very well on animals.

Make sure to reward your dog in a manner appropriate to the task he is expected to perform.

If you want your dog to behave well, he will need to internalize good behavior. This simply means that good behavior will seem to come naturally to your dog rather than it having to be reinforced. Punishment makes this difficult or impossible because punishment is pain (either physical or psychological), and pain sets up barriers to internalization.

For example, let's say your dog does something you don't like, such as snapping at a visitor. Yelling at or striking him creates an immediate unpleasant association in his mind between the stimulus (the visitor) and the punishment. He will associate pain with visitors, and that will not make him like your guests any better.

Punishment also has other drawbacks: Its effectiveness is temporary, it gives an unclear message (you are telling the dog what not to do but not what to do instead), and it may frighten the dog. Don't get me wrong—punishment may stop the behavior you are trying to extinguish. However, I can guarantee you that same behavior will pop up again in

Quick Tip

Hold at least two training sessions every day while you are working on a new skill.

the future because you haven't helped the dog solve the problem.

Use a Forceful Tone, Never Force

You don't have to punish your dog to get him to behave. (That's why they make dog biscuits.) Using physical punishment is almost always a mistake and almost always avoidable. Most of the time, a dark tone of voice, threatening body posture, and a hard stare is sufficient. These are much more important than any words you might say.

Why Punishment Fails

Let's say your dog jumps up on you. You yell angrily at him. This is intended as punishment, and it's true that most dogs do not like to be yelled at. However, the dog may see the attention he's getting as enough of an encouragement to keep doing it anyway because most dogs like any attention (as long as it's not actually painful) better than no attention. In addition, yelling at a dog raises his excitement level and makes it harder for him to listen to what you want him to do.

Make It Easy: Vocal Tones

Although human beings are capable of an almost unlimited vocal range, novice trainers should use only three basic tones for dog training:

- **The command tone.** Speak in a firm, clear, expectant tone. ("Sit, Dodger!")
- **The praise tone.** This is the light, happy voice you use to reward your dog for good work. ("Good boy, Samson!")
- **The corrective tone.** Use this dark, stern voice to let your dog know that he is making a big mistake. ("No bark, Bailey!")

If you catch your dog getting into mischief, or wish to correct a behavior, use a mild correction rather than stern punishment.

TRAINING EQUIPMENT

At the most basic level, all you really need to train a dog is the dog himself and some treats, but it has become customary over the years to add leashes and collars to the mix.

COLLAR

Your training collar should be a well-fitting regular buckle collar made of leather or nylon. You should be able to insert two fingers between the collar and the dog's neck. However, a collar that is too loose can be dangerous; it could get caught on something.

Some trainers may use choke chains and prong collars, but I don't like them as a rule. You should never have to physically harm your dog in any way, under any circumstances.

Dog collars play another very important purpose: They hold your dog's identification tags.

Head Halter

The head halter gives you more effective control over your dog than a standard collar does. It basically consists of one strap around the nose and another around the neck, behind the ears. Usually the neck strap must be as high up on the neck as you can get it, and you should be able to insert one finger between the strap and your dog's fur. A leash is attached to the halter under the chin via a ring. It works by putting firm but gentle pressure on the nose rather than by tugging on the neck as a regular collar does.

The greatest disadvantage of the head halter is that it should not be left on your dog while you're not around to supervise. It also can rub the hair off his nose. Most dogs don't really like them but will accustom themselves to them over time.

If you decide to use a head halter, follow the instructions that come with the package to help you fit and use it properly.

Front-Loop Harness

Unlike a regular harness, a front-loop harness has an attachment for the leash just below the sternum. The front-loop harness does not set up an oppositional reflex but allows even a child to gently lead a strong dog. It's easy to put on the dog, can remain on for an

Both you and your dog may benefit from professional help when training.

extended period, and is comfortable.

This is the ideal tool for a leisurely walk because it allows the dog to sniff about but still gives you total control. When the dog starts to drift away, a gentle tug of the lead brings him back again. The front-loop harness also does not require extensive practice the way a head halter does.

LEASH
Any well-stocked pet supply store offers a dazzling array of leashes, but not all of them are suitable for training. The so-called retractable lead, for example, which allows your dog to wander around rather freely for 10 or 15 feet (3 or 4.6 m), is not a proper training tool. Instead, select a 6-foot-long (1.8-m-long) sturdy leash made of leather, heavy cotton, or parachute strapping. Nylon leashes are cheapest, but I don't recommend them because they can really dig into your hand. If you have a big dog, pick a leash that is about 1 inch (2.5 cm) wide; a smaller dog does fine on a leash 1/2 inch (1.3 cm) wide.

REWARDS
Rewards, usually in the form of food treats, are your single best tool for training your dog, although some dogs seem to crave praise or playtime almost as much.

Quick Tip

Don't use a retractable lead with a head halter; it can be dangerous.

Treats should be plentiful, small (pea-sized), tasty, healthy, and readily available. Choose a treat that your dog likes but not too much; save the things he's absolutely wild over for emergency situations (like trading for your expensive wallet). If he likes the treat *too* much, he will concentrate on the reward rather than on what you are trying to teach him. On the other hand, if the reward is something he gets all the time anyway, he is unlikely to show sufficient motivation for training. This is really something you are going to have to discuss with your dog.

FORMAL TRAINING: DOG SCHOOL

If this is your first experience training a dog, do yourself and him a huge favor and take him to training classes.

Make It Easy: Socialization

Properly socializing your dog is just as important as formal training. The key socialization period in your dog's life occurs before he is 16 to 18 weeks old. This is the time for him to meet all kinds of new people and be exposed to different environments. The more things your puppy is exposed to, the calmer and more confident he will be as he grows up. Here's a quick checklist of "socialization targets" for your puppy:

• 100 human beings of all ages and both sexes. The list should include disabled people; people with canes; loud, boisterous people; babies; joggers; people on bikes; people in weird hats and uniforms; bearded people; bespectacled people; people carrying packages; people pushing baby carriages; and so on.

• Other dogs of both sexes and of all ages, sizes, and breeds.

• Cats, livestock, birds, and small pets. Some breeds with high prey drives cannot be trusted unsupervised around small pets.

• Strange environments, like shopping areas; friends' houses; the country; bridges; tunnels; barns; the city; and so on. Use your imagination.

This is to train you as much as it is to train the dog.

Don't expect a dog training class to instantly solve your problems, but it will lay a solid foundation for solving them over time. Studies have shown that puppies who have had obedience classes with other puppies have fewer problem behaviors than those without any training.

What Your Dog (and You) Will Learn

The best obedience courses for puppies, sometimes called puppy kindergarten, are group classes where you will participate with other dogs and their owners. Your puppy will learn how to socialize with other dogs, how to cope with distractions, and how to accept you as a reliable trainer. Most classes run about an hour and continue for six to eight weeks. Choose a course that covers all the basics and that uses the reward method to train your dog, not one that relies on punishment or heavy correction. A good course also will provide you with homework between classes to keep both you and your dog focused.

You also may decide to do some individual training; in most cases, the trainer will come to your home. But remember that anybody can call herself a dog trainer— no state requires a license for the job.

Where to Find Professional Help

Start with a recommendation for a course or trainer from someone you trust, such as your veterinarian or a member of your local kennel club or breed club. Your local humane society also may have some recommendations. The Association of Pet Dog Trainers (APDT) is also a wonderful place to start looking for a good teacher for your precious pooch.

Always remember that while training a dog requires some work, it's nothing compared to the grief that is sure to come if you allow your dog to run your life. A trained dog is a happy dog—and one who brings happiness to others.

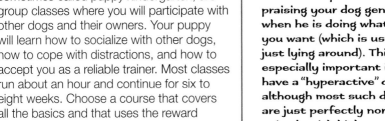

Quick Tip

Praise your dog for behaving well, not just when he does what you ask but in general. For instance, we are accustomed to reprimanding a dog for barking but saying nothing when he is quiet. Practice praising your dog gently when he is doing what you want (which is usually just lying around). This is especially important if you have a "hyperactive" dog— although most such dogs are just perfectly normal animals with high exercise requirements.

Quick
&Easy

Chapter 2

Crate Training

rate training helps your dog to be comfortable and happy in an enclosure designed to be his own personal space, or "den," and is an important part of modern dog ownership. Dogs who are properly crate trained can be transported in comfort and safety, confined for their own protection while recovering from surgery, or kept safe from chaos while the house is being remodeled. The crate is also a comfortable, safe, clean place for the dog to escape to when he needs a quiet snooze away from kids, cats, or other dogs in the house. It also serves as a housetraining aid.

Quick Tip

If your dog is a chewer, opt for a crate with a steel rather than a plastic pan.

CHOOSING THE RIGHT CRATE

Crate types include plastic, wire, and soft-sided. The wire crate allows more ventilation, but the solid plastic crate makes some dogs feel safer. The soft-sided crates are light, airy and easy to handle, but are not as secure as the other types. All three types are available in a choice of colors.

Good plastic dog crates:
- are made of durable polypropylene
- have ventilation side panels and a leak-proof bottom that also can be used alone as a pet bed
- can be assembled without tools in a short time
- are great for housetraining puppies
- provide privacy and safety
- are the only type approved for airline travel

Good wire dog crates:
- are easy to clean
- have a pan (plastic or steel) that slides out for easy maintenance
- provide maximum ventilation
- if portable, can fold down for easy storage

Good soft-sided crates:
- are extremely portable and lightweight
- are easy to store
- have a convenient carrying handle
- can be set up in a matter of seconds
- are made of durable, waterproof materials such as nylon
- have a cover for rainy weather

It's also a good idea to get a crate pad. There are plenty of designs available, but choose something that is machine washable, fast drying, and that has a stain-release finish. Good crate pads also have a nonslip backing.

SIZE

Just as important as the type of crate is its size. The general rule is to choose a crate that is big enough for your dog to stand up straight, turn around, and lie stretched out in, with enough room for a water bowl as well. If the crate is the correct size and the puppy is not crated for too long, he will not eliminate in his crate, especially if you

Did You Know?

A crate also can be called a cage—but it's not a prison.

make sure that he has "gone" before you put him in there.

COOLING THE CRATE

In hot weather, a crate fan will provide needed airflow, which is especially important for traveling pets. Fans circulate the air, removing warm air from the cage interior, and can help to protect your pet from overheating. Most are quiet, two-speed, and battery powered. Many feature a built-in thermometer to measure ambient temperature, as well as a port to accommodate an AC/DC adapter. You also can buy a freezer pack to help to cool your dog.

HOW TO CRATE TRAIN

Place the crate in an inhabited part of the house, not in the cellar, garage, or spare bedroom. Your puppy needs a place of his own, but he also needs to be around people. At night, the

A crate provides your dog with a safe, comfortable place he can call his own.

Make It Easy: Choosing a Crate

Here are some approximate crate sizes for popular breeds:

- **Toy breeds (Maltese, Toy Poodles, Yorkshire Terriers): small**
- **Miniature Schnauzers and Parson Russell Terriers: medium or small**
- **Most spaniels and Shelties: medium**
- **Siberian Huskies, small Labradors, small Golden Retrievers: large**
- **Larger retrievers, setters, German Shepherd Dogs, Rottweilers: very large**
- **Giant breeds (Newfoundlands, Great Danes, Mastiffs): extra large**

Some dogs will take more quickly to their crates than others.

Did You Know?

Anything over 55°F (12.8°C) in the sun is warm weather to a dog. Short-nosed breeds like the Pekingese and heavily coated or Arctic breeds like Siberian Huskies suffer most, but no dog can remain comfortable in the blazing sun for long. Dogs are animals who don't have an efficient cooling system—panting just doesn't work all that well. Please don't leave an unsupervised crated dog on a terrace, roof, or especially inside a car during warm weather.

crate should be in your bedroom, right next to you.

Some puppies take to a crate immediately; others do not. To introduce a reluctant dog to the crate, place an old towel down for bedding and add a few of your puppy's favorite toys and treats at the far end of the crate. If he is very nervous, you can start putting the treats by the door and gradually move them toward the back. Leave the door open. You may have to tie the crate door back so that it stays open without moving or closing. If the crate comes with a floor pan that rattles and scares the dog, put a piece of cardboard or a towel between the pan and the floor.

If you have a plastic crate, take it apart by removing the top and the door. Let your dog go freely in and out of the bottom half of the crate; when he gets

used to this procedure, reattach the top half. This process may require anywhere from several hours to a few days. (This step can be omitted in the case of a young puppy who accepts crating right away.)

The puppy likely will find his way into the crate quickly. At the start of training, praise and pet your dog when he enters. Never push or pull him into the crate. If you terrify him at this stage, he could develop a barrier anxiety that will stay with him forever. Eventually he will be quite comfortable coming and going.

The next step is to feed your dog in the crate with the door closed. Once he is comfortable taking his meal inside the crate, try putting him in there for his nap. Watch him carefully, and harden your heart if he barks to be let out. If you give in to that, there will be no end of it. (You can offer him a treat or chew to make his stay more comfortable, however.)

Quick Tip

It's smart to remove your dog's collar before crating him. Even a buckle collar could get entangled in the crate's bars. If you feel nervous about having no identification on your dog, such as when you are traveling, use a safety or "breakaway" collar. Breakaway collars have special buckles that are designed to snap when enough pressure is put on them from various directions.

As soon as he wakes up from his nap, take him outside immediately for a potty break. Once your dog can nap comfortably and quietly in his crate, congratulations! He has been crate trained.

It is commonly said that a puppy can stay in a crate for one hour for every month of his age, plus one. In other words, a four-month-old puppy can be in a crate for five hours. This is ridiculous. No puppy ever should be in a crate for that length of time unless it is nighttime and he is asleep. Unless the dog is recovering from surgery, traveling in a plane, or something truly extraordinary is going on, a couple of hours is more than enough time for anyone to spend in a crate. Life is too short to be shut up in a crate for hours on end.

THE CRATE AND PUNISHMENT

A crate should never be used for punishment—although a quick "time-out" may be useful to calm your dog down when he gets overly excited or too nippy. Do not leave your dog in a crate while you go to work. Crated dogs get bored, anxious, and destructive after a couple of hours and ideally only should be crated when you are home.

Your dog should see his crate as a "safe house,"

No dog should be confined to his crate for more than a few hours at a time.

not a place of exile. Let children know that the crate is the puppy's personal space and should be respected. Never allow a child to play in the dog's crate. Children also should be forbidden to handle the dog while he is in his safe place.

CRATE PROBLEM BEHAVIORS

In a perfect world, your dog would take to his crate immediately without any trouble at all. (This does actually happen in some cases.) However, assuming your world isn't perfect, here are some potential problems you may encounter when crate training—and what to do about them.

ACCIDENTS

If your puppy has a housetraining accident in the crate, just wash it out using a pet odor neutralizer. Don't use an ammonia-based product because the odor resembles urine and may encourage your dog to make the same mistake again. Don't scold him unless you actually catch him in the act of eliminating.

BARKING

If your dog barks a lot in his crate, the cause could be one of several things. Some dogs, like terriers, are just vocal. If your dog barks both in and out of his crate, you obviously can't blame the crate for the disturbance. Dogs also may bark in their crates if they are bored, underexercised, or anxious. It is important to discover why your dog is barking and treat the underlying problem.

CHEWING

Some dogs, when bored or anxious, may begin chewing on their crates. This is especially likely to happen if your dog is suffering from separation anxiety; dogs with

Quick Tip

Don't crate a dog who is vomiting or has diarrhea, or one who has had insufficient exercise.

this condition often develop "barrier anxiety"and actually get worse when closely confined.

Although a good crate will stand up to almost anything, your dog can injure his teeth in the process of chewing on his crate. If your dog is chewing out of boredom but absolutely must be crated, supply him with a peanut butter-filled chew toy to exercise those restless jaws. If he has separation anxiety, there are procedures and medications that can help—talk with your veterinarian.

USING A CRATE WISELY

Once you and your dog get used to the idea of a crate, you both will find it a convenient and useful addition to your lives. But remember, your dog is a living, breathing creature who needs to explore his world—most of the problems people have with their dogs are simply due to the fact that the dog is not getting enough exercise.

Crates are an important tool. They are a safe den, a sleeping compartment, and maybe even a dining room. However, they are not jails or long-term puppy-sitters. Please use them wisely.

Chapter 3

Housetraining

Housetraining is simply teaching your dog the habit of going outdoors or to another owner-designated spot to eliminate, rather than on the floor. Dogs housetrain fairly easily, which is one reason why they have become house pets rather than barnyard animals. However, some training is still required.

Unlike cats, who usually just have to be shown a litter box, dogs needs a little tutoring to get the right idea. A dog is considered housetrained when he has no accidents for several months (unless he is ill or you have been gone for an unconscionably long period).

Most dogs can be taught to eliminate outdoors fairly easily.

HOW TO HOUSETRAIN

Housetraining can be made very simple using a process of containment, relocation, attention, patience, and scheduling. (All of these are things that *you* have to do. You're the owner, after all.)

CONTAINMENT

Dogs are clean animals by instinct and do not wish to soil their own living quarters, so you need to set up a "living area" for your dog. This area is *separate* from his crate, although the crate can be included in the area. I prefer to use a larger area than the crate alone for housetraining purposes, because while a dog occasionally needs to be confined, he also needs room to move around.

Use a small, tiled room such as a bathroom or part of the kitchen, and put a comfortable bed (or your dog's crate) in there. The living area should be small enough so that it easily confines the dog but large enough for him to eat and play

Did You Know?

If your dog continues to use his living area as a toilet area, you may need to make it smaller or take him outside more frequently.

there—and for you to go and join him.

Don't Make Him "Hold It"

Never confine your dog to his living area for too long. Puppies less than four months old have weak sphincter muscles and can't be expected to "hold it" for more than a couple of hours. A dog needs to eliminate about as often as a person does—and puppies need to eliminate as often as babies do. Even dogs who succeed in "holding it" put themselves at risk of developing urinary infections and bladder stones from doing so.

Quick Tip

Never withhold water from your dog in an effort to housetrain him more quickly. This is both cruel and dangerous.

Keep Your Eyes Open

While your dog is in the housetraining stage, he should be in his den, in his crate, on a leash, or under your watchful eye at all times. Dogs do not like to soil their sleeping quarters, and if you learn the signs of impending elimination, such as pacing, circling, and uneasiness, it's easy to slip him quickly out the door.

You also can tether your dog to your belt while you go about your daily tasks. This gives him more exercise, enables you to watch for signs that he needs to "go," and also acts as a bonding experience for you and your dog. It's a bit of a chore, but if you do it right, he will housetrain quickly, and that's a better deal than mopping the floor for the next eight months.

RELOCATION

This doesn't mean that you are going to move soon; it means that you are going to give your dog a special outdoor toilet area. This helps him remember to "go" when he reaches the right spot (the smell that remains from previous eliminations, fortunately undetectable by you, also will give him a clue). Every time your dog needs to eliminate, take him to this prearranged spot. Go with your dog—don't just let him out. Although you will want to keep this area clean, it doesn't hurt to leave one or two little "reminders" to clue your dog in as to why he is there.

Location, Location, Location

You want to make sure that your dog actually eliminates, and you want to get him in the habit of using a particular area, not just anywhere outside (like right in front of the door). This is for your own benefit, of course. If the toilet

 **Quick Tip**

If your dog soils his bed, it could be a sign of a urinary tract infection or other medical problem.

area you have chosen is rather distant from the house, your small puppy may not make it there in time. To speed things up, you may have to carry him to the spot or maybe pick a place that's a little closer.

However, don't let your dog think that there is only one place he can ever go—this also can create problems. Encourage him to use a designated area, but don't insist on it. If you do, he may be reluctant to "go," even if he needs to while on a walk away from his regular spot. When he gets home, it's too late, and there's only one place left—your floor.

Why Won't He Go?

One problem that sometimes occurs when housetraining is that the dog fails to "perform" when on his walk but immediately eliminates upon returning to the house. There can be several explanations for this seemingly paradoxical behavior. For example, the dog may be so excited by his trip outdoors that he has forgotten why he's out there and only remembers upon returning to the house, when it's too late.

Pick a general spot for your dog to eliminate in, but don't use the same location all the time.

The secret, of course, is to make sure that you have your dog out long enough. Puppies especially may need to eliminate more than once during an outing. Don't assume that one urination and one defecation are "it." Sometimes, on the other hand, the puppy won't go at all. This may be because he remembers that in the past, the minute his mission was accomplished, you took him right back in the house instead of allowing him to have some outdoor playtime. Always let the bathroom trip be accompanied by at least a little play!

A different problem can be presented by a dog who was inhumanely housetrained in the past. If a dog was punished for going in the house, he may remember only that eliminating is an act frowned upon by his owner—not that it's wrong to go in the house. If that is the case, the dog may hesitate to perform in front of his owner and instead may wait until he gets home so that he can hide it.

Quick Tip

Some breeds of dog, such as toy breeds and hounds, may take longer to housetrain than others. Be patient. If you are having trouble, despite your best efforts, consult a veterinarian to see if he has a medical problem, such as a bladder infection.

ATTENTION

All dogs give signals when they are ready to eliminate, and it is your responsibility to figure out what your dog's signal is. He may whine, go to the door, circle, lick his nose, sniffle, or do something else to show you he has an urgent need to go. Not all dogs give the same signal, but if you keep your puppy close by your side, you soon will learn what his private code is. Your puppy is too young to understand that this is something he needs to communicate to you. Sometimes you can establish a signal yourself; some people have hooked up bells to their door that their dogs rather quickly learned to ring when they wanted to go outside.

PATIENCE

Don't expect your dog to master housetraining in a few days—although it may indeed work out that way with some dogs. (How long did it take you to be toilet trained?) The more patient you are, the less stress is in the air and the faster your puppy will get trained.

SCHEDULING

Scheduling doesn't necessarily refer to clock watching; it also refers to your dog's activities. In other words, puppies

Quick &Easy Well-Behaved Family Dog

Your dog may give signals that he needs to eliminate, such as whining or standing by the door.

often have to eliminate right after eating, sleeping, and playing—not at 12 o'clock, 2 o'clock, and 4 o'clock. Keep your dog on a regular feeding schedule. This not only makes elimination patterns more regular but also will make the puppy less anxious and more assured about his dinner. A less anxious puppy is less apt to urinate or defecate inappropriately. It also helps to feed your puppy premium, highly digestible puppy food. This will make his stools firmer and less messy.

OTHER TRAINING METHODS

Alternative housetraining methods include paper training and litter training.

PAPER TRAINING

While some people paper train their dogs successfully, most of the time, paper training is counterproductive. First, it adds an unnecessary step, and second, it may backfire. Why? Because you're teaching your dog to eliminate in the house, not outside. It is often difficult for dogs to distinguish between the right place to eliminate and the wrong one. (For very small dogs in high-rise apartments, however, paper training may be useful.)

LITTER TRAINING

One of the latest trends is litter training small dogs. It really does work and is very convenient if you live in an upper-level apartment or are gone for a large part of the day. Some of these systems actually function like an indoor toilet and come in two parts: a tray and a grid. The grid drains away the urine and allows it to collect at the bottom of the tray. Solid waste can be removed easily as well.

However, as with paper training, a potential problem with litter training is that it breaks the taboo of not peeing indoors. Some dogs get very careless over time about this and start eliminating everywhere. Also, because it really isn't natural for dogs to eliminate inside, don't expect litter training a dog to be as easy as litter training a cat. Put the litter tray in a marginal area of the house, such as a utility or laundry room. (Besides, who wants a litter tray in the kitchen?)

Also, always remember that litter training is not an excuse not to go outside with your dog to let him explore the wide world out there.

POTENTIAL HOUSETRAINING PROBLEMS

Here are some of the problems you may encounter while housetraining your dog, as well as solutions for them.

ACCIDENTS

When your dog makes a mistake, don't reprimand him. That only confuses him—he doesn't know why you're scolding him and may think that he's in trouble for eliminating at all. Because he can't stop eliminating, he will then be forced to hide it.

Solution

If you actually catch your dog in the act of having an accident, pick him up and scurry him outside, saying "Outside!" Never strike your dog, and never rub his nose in an accident. This kind of behavior is humiliating for a dog and disrupts the positive relationship you want to create with him. You will be making the problem worse instead of better. Would you hit a child who was slow to potty train? Of course not.

If your puppy has a tail, tuck it between his legs as you carry him out to the backyard. That may help. Once you are outside with him, stay with him. Do not abandon him to wander (and wonder) in the backyard.

Too Late? Too Bad!

If you come upon an accident after the fact…too bad. You should have been watching your dog more carefully. There is nothing you can do to correct him at this point. If you yell at a dog after an accident, he will have no idea why you are screaming. The next thing you know, you will have a terrified dog. Simply clean up the accident and go on with your life.

> ### Did You Know?
>
> You can help to relocate your dog's toilet area by buying special toilet stakes impregnated with a urine scent (you can't smell it) that encourages the dog to pee against the stake.

Make It Easy: Cleaning Up

If your dog has an accident (and he will), it's important to remove all traces of the urine. If you don't, he will be tempted to return to the same spot because the smell of urine reminds him every time he passes that this is a good place to eliminate. If it's fresh urine, clean the rug with a good carpet shampoo. However, if the urine has penetrated through the rug to the pad beneath, it's unlikely you'll be able to remove it completely. Good odor removers are manufactured especially for dealing with doggy accidents and contain enzymes to break down the odor-causing compounds in urine and feces. Follow the directions carefully, and let the cleaner soak in as deeply as the urine itself. You will have to keep the spot warm and wet for 24 hours. It also helps to cover the area with plastic during this period.

EXCITEMENT URINATION

Young dogs often lack sufficient bladder control to keep from "peeing their pants" at the thrill of seeing you again. This is quite normal behavior and will cure itself over time. Most of the time, the puppy is probably not even aware that he is urinating.

Solution

Don't punish, scold, or correct the behavior; calmly ignore it. You can help to prevent the situation from developing by being calm yourself when you come home. If you feed into your dog's excitement, you'll just make the problem worse. Simply walk in the house without greeting your dog, and keep yourself occupied away from him for a few minutes. When he has calmed down, you can cuddle him and tell him how much you missed him all day.

SUBMISSIVE URINATION

Submissive urination is a spontaneous, unintentional release of urine. It is a sign of insecurity and occurs as a gesture of appeasement to a dominant being perceived by the dog as threatening. (That's you.) This is a problem often seen with abused or very shy young dogs who have not yet learned more socially acceptable ways to show their respect.

Solution

To correct the behavior, just ignore it completely. Don't try to reassure him because that will make him think that he is being praised for the behavior. Scolding him will make him feel worse and will increase the chances of it happening again.

Don't greet your dog when you enter the room or even make eye contact. By not looking, you are signaling to him that you are not a threat. As you bustle around the room, you can talk quietly to him. When you do pet him, kneel down next to him and pet him on the chest, not the top of the head. Head petting signifies dominance, and what you want is to build up your shy dog's confidence.

Submissive dogs do best with a consistent schedule. This gives them confidence because they know what is going to happen next. All important activities should be included in the schedule—especially mealtime, walk time, and playtime, all of which have a significant physical and psychological role in elimination.

Another thing that helps a dog with submissive urination is to learn a few simple obedience commands such as *sit*, *shake hands*, *down*, and *stay*. Obedience lessons build a dog's confidence and give him a sense of accomplishment.

Did You Know?

If you have a secure fence and a good neighborhood, consider installing a doggy door. This is merely a hinged flap (usually made of soft vinyl) set into a door, wall, or window to allow your dog to come and go freely. Doggy doors give the dog more control of his own elimination and can reduce scratching at the door, whining, and worst of all, eliminating in the house.

THE IMPORTANCE OF HOUSETRAINING

It shouldn't be necessary to explain why housetraining is important. It's obvious that a house that is free of urine and dog stools is more attractive, pleasanter, and healthier than the opposite. Lack of housetraining is also one of the most common reasons people give for surrendering their pets to a shelter. The efforts you make in housetraining your dog are well worth the rewards.

Never punish your dog for an accident indoors, especially if you do not catch him in the act.

Chapter 4

Basic Commands for Good Behavior

Training is more than a way to get your dog to follow commands; it also provides him with company, attention, stimulation, and leadership. It's a dog's dream come true, and it's such an important part of dog ownership that you have to make time in your life to accomplish it, no matter how busy you are. If you are too busy to train a dog, you are too busy to own a dog.

MAKE TIME FOR TRAINING

Do you have a full schedule? The first thing you should do is to reset your alarm clock. Get up one hour earlier than you do now, and take your dog for a walk around the block or a run in the park. (Or if you have children, make them do it.) A walk provides your dog with exercise, mental stimulation, companionship, and training all at once.

When you want your dog to learn something new, however, you should begin teaching him indoors. When training outside, use a 6-foot (1.8 m) leash. Don't try to do too much, especially on the first day: Five minutes of training a day is about right for puppies, but older dogs can concentrate for about ten minutes when they are learning something new. Keep a slow and steady pace while training, and if either you or your dog begins to get tired or bored, quit and do something fun instead.

Be sure to vary the time of day when you train your dog. If you only train in the morning, your dog may get it into his head that he can behave as he likes during the afternoon. Dogs are odd creatures that way!

BASIC COMMANDS

The following are some relatively simple commands that your dog should learn.

WATCH ME

Watch me is the first, most basic command to teach your dog. Its purpose is to get him to pay attention to you—if he's not paying attention, he can't learn. When you teach this command, you are teaching him that important and pleasurable things will happen if he is on the ball.

How to Teach *Watch Me*

To teach the *watch me* command, use a high-value aromatic treat like a bit of liver or hot dog.
1. Hold the treat in front of your dog's nose, and then say "Watch me" while you place the treat under your own chin.

2. When he looks up expectantly, praise him and hand him the treat.
3. Start playing with him quietly, and then try the *watch me* command again. Soon your dog will figure out that "Watch me" means a reward is coming. Once your dog gets good at this, continue to practice the command around an increasing number of distractions.
4. After your dog has learned the command, start giving the treats intermittently. At other times, just praise him for obeying the command.
5. Finally, begin to wean the pup from the treats and simply praise him for looking

Quick Tip

Always end every practice on a positive note, even if you have to go back to a simpler exercise. Also, it bears repeating: Praise your dog when he does the right thing. This can't be overstated. Be lavish in your praise to your dog. It gets results.

The *watch me* command keeps your dog's attention focused on you to make teaching other commands easier.

Quick Tip

It's best to work on only one new command per week. While dogs aren't stupid, it's not wise to confuse them, either. Teaching *sit* and *down* in the same week is like teaching an elementary school student decimals and fractions at the same time.

when commanded. In no time at all you will be able to have his attention, no matter what he is doing.

Remember that different dogs learn at different rates and to keep training sessions short. The most important thing is for you and your dog to be having a great time with each other.

LEAVE IT
This is an important command, because you never know when your dog will get hold of something truly disgusting or harmful.

How to Teach *Leave It*
Start teaching this command with a small, fairly low-value treat like a bit of kibble.

1. Place the treat under your foot so that the dog can smell it but can't really grab it.
2. While he's sniffing around the treat, say "Leave it!"
3. When he looks up at you, reward him with a better treat. If he tries to grab the treat, just cover it again.
4. As training progresses, you can make the treat under your foot more visible, or use something more desirable to the dog. Eventually, he should be able to leave a high-value treat on the floor on command.

COME
The *come* command is one of the most important commands of all. Its purpose is to have a dog stop whatever he is doing and immediately return to you. This is especially useful if your dog is ever in danger.

How to Teach *Come*
You'll need a friend's help to teach your dog this command.

1. Start indoors in a safe area, with one of you holding the dog's leash.
2. The other person should hold a food reward so the dog can see it, back up about 10 feet (3 m), and then call him by name: "Roger, come!" (Of course, if the dog's name happens not to be Roger, use his own name instead.) You also can use a long leash to draw the dog to you.
3. When he approaches, praise him enthusiastically.
4. As your dog perfects this exercise, you can

The *come* command is particularly important because it may get your dog out of dangerous situations.

increase the distance between you, as well as the amount of distraction around the dog, by practicing in different and more exciting places. Dogs aren't very good at generalizing and may not understand that what works in the kitchen is also supposed to work outside in the world. Expect to "reteach" this command in many different areas and on many different surfaces, like grass, sand, dirt, concrete, and so forth.

How reliable your dog is when performing this command may be partially determined by genetics. Retrievers, for example, who are specifically bred to come back to their owners, are generally more adept at the *come* command than other breeds. Hounds, on the other hand, who were bred to follow their

Quick Tip

It's best to use small treats when training. You can choose anything that your dog likes: cheese, tiny hot dog slices, freeze-dried liver, hamburger, or even dog biscuits broken into small pieces.

Did You Know?

There is a difference between a bribe and a reward. A bribe is given in advance to get your dog to do something. (Some people call a bribe a "lure" because they think it sounds better, but a dog doesn't care.) A reward is given after the dog has performed his task correctly. Dogs like bribes and rewards equally well, I think.

noses (and then have you follow them), can be very unreliable off lead.

Of course, any dog can become distracted if the opposing stimulus is strong enough. What qualifies as a strong stimulus also depends on the breed. For example, if a Beagle sees a rabbit, he is probably going to run after it, no matter what you have to offer. Or given a chance to dine on their favorite food, most dogs won't come to you until they have finished, regardless of breed.

SIT

Sit is an important command. It can be used to quiet your dog when he is overexcited or as a prelude to teaching other commands, such as *wait* or *stay*. The *sit* is also the best position for your dog to be in while you're cleaning his ears or clipping his nails and is an important command when you're dealing with a dog with dominance issues. Lucky for you and your dog, he already knows how to sit. The trick is to make him sit on command, which isn't very difficult.

How to Teach *Sit*

1. Take a treat and hold it above your dog's nose, say "Sit" in a calm voice, and then slowly move it backward over his head.
2. As he follows the treat with his eyes, he will naturally plant his rump on the floor. Give a younger dog between 15 and 30 seconds to comply; an older dog who has already learned the command should respond within 5 seconds.
3. When your dog sits correctly, give him a treat immediately, by which I mean within three seconds at the most. Any longer than that and the dog either will forget why you are rewarding him at all or will associate the reward with a subsequent behavior, like standing up after the sit. If your dog does not sit after being given the command, ignore the behavior and try again a few seconds later.
4. Repeat the process a few times in a single session. After several sessions, you can use the treats more intermittently as a reward. Continue the training

using varying levels of distraction until you have a reliable sit. Soon your dog will be sitting on command.

If your dog fails to sit, do not repeat the command. Stop the exercise for a few minutes and come back to it later. He'll soon figure out that to get the reward he will need to perform the *sit*. There is also no need to push his butt down in a display of superior force.

Always use the same single-word command, and try not to say "Sit down," which the dog will confuse with the *down* command. The intricacies of the English language are hard enough for humans, let alone the family pet!

To check to see if your dog really understands what you are saying, practice giving commands in different body positions. He should be able to sit on command, even if your back is turned to him—or you're lying in bed. You shouldn't always have to tower over your dog and menace him. Eventually, you also should be able to use different tones of voice, including a whisper.

Sit is one of the most basic commands to teach your dog and serves as the foundation for several other commands and tricks.

STAY

Stay is the command you use to keep your dog in one place. (It is useful to keep him away from the door when someone is bringing in the groceries, for example.) Some trainers don't use this command at all because they feel that "sit" means "sit until you are told to get up," which is essentially the same thing. They feel that it is simpler to train the dog that way. However, the *stay* command gives the dog the psychological cue that he will be staying put for a longer time than in a typical sit.

How to Teach *Stay*
1. Get a short lead and attach it to your dog.
2. Give the sit command and praise him when he

43

complies. A dog can hold a stay from any position, but most people tend to begin teaching their dog to stay from a sitting position.

3. With your palm held out in a "stop" gesture (which dogs seem to understand instinctively), back up slowly, saying "Stay."
4. If he does indeed stay, praise him and give him a treat. Be sure to keep your praise low-key. Too much enthusiastic encouragement, including petting, will encourage him to get up.
5. When your dog seems to get it, begin increasing the length of time he is in the stay, gradually working up to five minutes. Then try it outdoors in a fenced, secure area. Eventually, your dog should be able to hold a stay for as long as 30 minutes.

If your dog doesn't stay, say nothing but quietly move him back to his original position and start again. Move only a short distance (two or three steps) away from him each time.

DOWN

Down is another important command, especially if you own a larger dog. Having your dog in a long *down* while you eat supper, for example, keeps his nose on the floor and not nudging against your plate.

For some dogs, *down* is a difficult skill to master. Lying down is a position of great vulnerability for a dog, so a dominant dog will be slower to down than a more submissive one.

Did You Know?

Be aware of contradictions in your tone, body language, and the words you use. They should all be saying the same thing, or at least not contradicting each other. You should never use a sweet sappy voice to say "No!" and your body language should remain authoritative. In the same way, towering over a dog and telling him in a loud, hard voice to relax is not going to have the desired effect. At best, you will confuse the dog. At worst, he'll misunderstand and do the opposite of what you want.

How to Teach *Down*

1. To lure your dog into the *down* position, hold a high-value treat near his nose.
2. Say "Down," and move your hand with the treat down between his forefeet.
3. He should lie down naturally to follow the treat. Praise him when he does so.

HEEL

Nothing is more pleasurable than a relaxed stroll around the block with your faithful dog at your side. The *heel* command is used to encourage your dog to remain there—not lagging behind or plunging ahead. Remember, you are supposed to be the leader, and your dog is supposed to be the follower. To start to teach heel, all you need are plenty of soft treats and a 6-foot (1.8 m) leash.

How to Teach *Heel*

The key to teaching this command is to show your dog that it's always rewarding for him to stay close to you.

Down can be a difficult command for your dog to learn, especially if he is a more dominant breed.

1. Hold some yummy treats in your hand, right where you want your dog's nose to be.
2. If he begins to pull on his leash, stop, say "Wait," and then begin walking in another direction.
3. To help him out in this case, try to get him to calm down and relax: Give him the sit command and offer him a treat when he complies. Pet him and speak gently in a calming tone. It may take several minutes for your dog to calm down and sit quietly, but don't move a step until he does.
4. When he seems to relax, start walking. If he still pulls, repeat steps 1 and 2. This not only calms your dog but also teaches him that when he pulls on the leash he is not getting anywhere. Soon he will learn that the walk doesn't begin—or continue—while he is pulling.

Walk slowly and speak quietly to your dog. If you are excited and yell, he will respond with equal excitement. What you

Quick Tip

Practice the sit command right before your dog's dinnertime so that he's hungry and eager for a food reward.

45

The *heel* command teaches your dog to walk calmly at your side while on a leash.

are really doing here is helping him achieve some self-control. This is also a time to use the *watch me* command, to keep his attention focused on where it should be: you.

However, you don't want your dog to snap to a *heel* position every minute you are walking. It's important to take time now and again in the walk to let your dog sniff, stop, explore, and wander. Use the *heel* only when you want your dog to stay close at your side.

Why Your Dog Pulls on His Leash
Many times your dog is not willfully trying to disobey you when he pulls on the leash. Sometimes, he will

begin to yank on the lead the second it's attached to the collar out of sheer excitement. He is not trying to take control; he's just so enthused about the walk that he literally can't restrain himself.

Grabbing the leash fiercely to hold the dog in place shows only that you are stronger than he is and can forcefully restrain him. This is no help if a child is walking a dog; besides, a continual tug-of-war is no fun for either of you.

A DOG ON HIS BEST BEHAVIOR

Training benefits both owner and dog. A well-trained dog is a pleasure to be around and is likely to be welcomed everywhere he goes. For the sake of your pet-owning future, take the time to train your dog—give him the chance to be the valuable companion he yearns to be.

Make It Easy: Holding a Leash

Holding a leash may seem simple, but doing it the wrong way will get the wrong response from your dog. Here's how to do it right, with your dog walking at your left side:

1. Hold your arms loosely in front of you with your palms facing in.
2. In your right hand, put the leash's loop over your thumb, with the loose end crossing your palm.
3. Fold the leash in an accordion-like way until it is at a suitable length.
4. The loose end should leave the right hand from under your pinkie.
5. With your other hand, make a loop of your thumb and index finger.
6. Run the leash through that loop and across your palm.
7. Wrap your other fingers loosely around the lead, which should leave your left hand from under the pinkie. You should have enough leash between your left hand and the collar to form a small loop.

This is called the "control" position, for the simple reason that it allows perfect control over your dog's movements. Your left hand will make a correction if necessary while your right hand will remain stationary.

Chapter 5

Training to Fix Problem Behaviors

Most dogs today are bored and understimulated. People leave their pets alone for long hours every day, and when they are home, they spend the evening watching television or surfing the Internet. It's a dull day for a dog, and with no one to pay attention to him, he is bound to get into trouble. He can't read, has no stamp collection, and probably is not allowed to go out visiting his friends. What your dog can do instead is chew, destroy the furniture, dig up the yard, and terrorize the cat.

You Know What Your Problem Is?

Almost all dog "problem behaviors" are normal canine behaviors that either happen at the wrong time or are directed at the wrong target. When most of us are talking about "dog problems" we really mean "people problems." And while dogs do have problems, they aren't the same ones people have. Here's a simple example: Let's say you come home from a hard day's work and find that your dog has torn the curtains, eaten your shoes, and peed on the rug. You definitely have a problem: a destructive dog. The dog has a problem too, but it's not destruction. It's boredom or loneliness.

Destroying your living room is your dog's way of dealing with his problem. The fact that he created a different problem for you is not his concern, and you will not be able to solve your destructive dog problem until you solve your dog's loneliness or boredom problem.

NO SUCH THING AS A GUILTY DOG

Dogs do not have a sense of morality. They do not feel guilt. What we often interpret as guilt is a foreboding they may feel that they are going to get into deep trouble. Dogs cannot commit sins. They can behave in ways that you don't like, but that doesn't make them morally reprehensible. Dogs are merely trying to get by in life. They wish to earn your approval (if you don't make that too hard), and they would like to be fed on time and be given a warm bed. They also need discipline, exercise, and attention. These are simple needs, but if they are not met, problem behaviors will result.

BEHAVIORAL PROBLEMS, MEDICAL CAUSES

If your dog is exhibiting problem behaviors, have your vet check him out before you tear your hair out trying to decide what you did wrong or plunk down a fortune in behavioral therapy. Problem behaviors can be caused by parasites, hearing or vision loss, endocrine or hormonal problems, thyroid dysfunction, Cushing's disease, hypersexuality, spinal problems, hyperactivity, medications, toxins,

If you want a better-behaved dog, give him more exercise—tired dogs are good dogs.

and a host of other possibilities. Other "problem" behaviors are really normal, ingrained dog behaviors and can only be managed rather than "cured."

ADDRESSING PROBLEM BEHAVIORS

Dogs are pretty simple creatures, and while they can exhibit an alarming variety of undesirable behavior, in most cases the cause is easy to discover and the behavior is curable. It takes commitment, but it can be done.

Left to their own devices, dogs will bite when annoyed, bark all night, pee anywhere they please, and chew anything that strikes their fancy. It is your job to steer them away from that natural behavior and to show them a better way.

The following are some behavioral problems you may encounter in your dog and advice on what you can do about them.

AGGRESSION

Aggression is violence or the threat of violence from your dog. It can include growling, snapping, and biting and can be directed to small animals, other dogs, strangers, or members of the family. Some kinds of aggression, such as that directed against small animals, are the result of a natural prey drive. This type of aggression is bred into certain dogs and is not possible to "cure." In this case, you must simply avoid letting your dog around cats or small pets. Other kinds of aggression can be the result of a physical problem, such as a brain tumor or thyroid disorder. Most aggression, however, stems from some kind of stress in the dog's life. Stressors can include insufficient leadership on the part of the owner, mistrust, and many other factors.

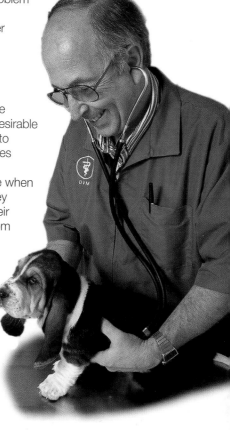

A veterinary examination may reveal a medical cause for your dog's problem behaviors.

SOLUTION

When dealing with an aggressive dog, don't pretend that the problem doesn't exist. Ignoring or making excuses for your dog's aggression will not make it go away. In fact, it probably will get worse. Get professional

Did You Know?

Certain behaviors such as pacing, jumping, and other obsessive actions can be reduced by providing a different feeding environment. Instead of slapping all the food down in a bowl and letting your dog eat it in 20 seconds, let him work for it. Satisfy his urge to hunt and solve problems. Use a feed hopper (a device that can dispense food at predetermined intervals) or stuffable toy, and hide the food in different places. Provide some opportunity for your dog to think rather than behave mindlessly.

help to solve this problem unless you are interested in a lawsuit (or permanent scarring). Talk to your veterinarian about getting in touch with a trainer or behaviorist who specializes in aggression issues. Aggression can be cured, but it takes a serious commitment on the part of both the family and a skilled trainer.

BARKING (EXCESSIVE)

Barking is a natural behavior. Most of the time, dogs bark to call our attention to something. (This is known as "alarm barking.") This kind of bark consists of a few short, sharp barks with short pauses between them.

SOLUTION

The best way to handle this kind of barking is to acknowledge the dog's intent. Don't just mindlessly say "Shut up, Shadow." Instead, walk to the window and examine the scene carefully. Let the dog see you doing this. When you see it's only old lady Seaborg and her Pomeranian, pat your dog's head and assure him "Thanks, Shadow. That's old lady Seaborg and her Pomeranian." If the dog barks at visitors, do basically the same thing: Call him over, thank him for noticing that someone has been pounding on the door for five minutes, and give him a treat.

Handling the Lonely Barker

Some dogs bark not to alert you to passersby or visitors but simply because they are bored and lonely. If you keep your dog in the yard all day and the neighbors mention that his continual barking is driving them crazy, you know that you have a bored dog.

The fact is that dogs need human companionship. If you're gone long hours every day, think about hiring the kid next door to walk your dog. Your dog will appreciate the attention and change of scenery, and the neighbors will appreciate the silence.

Sometimes you also can get a dog to be quiet by totally ignoring the behavior. However, that won't solve his original problem (boredom), and he may begin to

Excessive barking can be handled by acknowledging the cause and praising your dog for brief barking.

express himself in other equally undesirable ways, such as chewing the furniture or developing an obsessive-compulsive habit like tail chasing or repetitive paw licking.

BEGGING

Begging is a natural behavior. Wolves do it within their own pack, and so do both feral and domesticated dogs. They do it because it works: They look at you with those soft, large eyes and it's just easier to give in and hand over a piece of that boiled liver you didn't want anyway. Children are especially adept at passing over broccoli and other less-than-desirable food to their pets.

It is always tempting to make your dog happy by treating him to some of your dinner, but his happiness will soon turn into your everlasting regret. Once you start giving in to a begging dog, the behavior is very hard to extinguish. If you have not yet begun handing out parts of your dinner to the dog, good for you—don't start. However, if even one member of the family hands your dog a treat from her plate even one time, you have encouraged a habit that is going to be very hard to break.

SOLUTION

The way to stop begging is simply not to give in. Banish

Did You Know?

Not only is begging a bad and annoying habit, but some kinds of people food are toxic to dogs. Chocolate, onions, macadamia nuts, alcoholic beverages, grapes, and raisins are among the human foods that never should be given to a dog.

your dog from the room if you have to, but never feed him from the table, no matter how much he whines or begs or paws. Eventually he will stop, but the behavior will get worse before it gets better because he will try harder and harder to win you over. Grit your teeth and suffer. He must learn that the only way he gets a treat is when you are standing up and not eating your own food. If you want to give him some healthy leftovers, you can, but give them to him on his own plate, well after you have finished eating.

CHEWING

Chewing is a natural behavior, especially for puppies, so keep your dog's mouth busy to prevent damage to your shoes and furniture.

SOLUTION

Give your dog a "legal" chew to replace the forbidden items. Carefully examine what he likes to chew. If he is attracted to cloth, give him cloth toys, or if he can rip these apart in seconds, a strong knotted rope toy might work. Another good choice is a hollow rubber toy into which you can insert treats. The beauty of this toy is that it gives a puppy something to exercise his jaws with and can keep him entertained for a long time.

You also can buy various "no-chew" bitter-tasting sprays with which to anoint furniture and other chewable items to make them less appealing to your dog. However, some dogs just ignore the taste and chomp right through it.

CLIMBING ON FURNITURE

Some athletic and high-minded dogs like to get on the furniture. They see you sitting there and see no reason why they shouldn't as well. If you allow your dog to get on the furniture, that's fine, but even then he should do so only when invited. Otherwise he will be leaping up into your terrified Aunt Viola's lap at every opportunity.

SOLUTION

If your dog persists on getting up on the furniture,

attach a short lead to his collar. When he attempts to climb on the furniture without your permission, say "No!" Be firm but not angry. If he does not get off the couch immediately, walk over there, say "No!" and guide him down with the leash. Don't drag him off the couch, and don't make eye contact with him. Again, say "No!" The point is to make him *want* to get off the couch. When he does climb down, praise him.

DIGGING

Some dogs are natural diggers and some aren't, and there are a hundred different reasons why.

WHY DOGS DIG

Digging can be quite productive—for a dog, that is. For one thing, it helps him find interesting things buried in the ground or under snow. Hunting dogs, for instance, know that the best way to get a rabbit out of his hole is to dig him out. There is nothing mysterious about this. (Mugwump, our inimitable Basset Hound, was an expert mole hunter. She'd sniff along the ground, and then all of a sudden she'd start digging like a madwoman.)

Unspayed females are more likely to engage in digging than their spayed sisters; it's a form of nesting behavior. Dogs kept outside a great deal are also more prone to digging. They are lonely, anxious, and bored, and digging a hole is a good way to pass the time. The following are some other reasons why dogs dig.

To Hide Their Food

Some dogs have the urge to dig so that they can bury their food supply. In

Provide your dog with appropriate chew toys to prevent him from chewing less desirable objects.

Your dog only should climb up on your furniture if you invite him to do so.

the wild, wolves who couldn't consume their dinners all at once needed a secure hiding place from scavengers and other predators. The earth not only covers the food, but it also preserves it because it's generally a few degrees cooler than the surrounding air.

To Keep Cool
Sometimes dogs dig to find themselves a cool spot. There's nothing nicer on a hot summer day, apparently, than to hollow out a lovely soft bed of cool earth and go to sleep in it. If your dog digs a number of shallow holes, usually in the shade, that's the reason.

To Escape Confinement
Digging near a fence line is an indication that the dog may be trying to escape, while digging near the house may mean that he's lonely and desires your company.

To Redecorate
Sometimes dogs dig because they're just plain bored with the landscape and seek to enhance the attractions of their environment. There's some evidence that dogs watch their owners garden and seek to emulate this behavior, at least to the extent

they can. Besides, the recently worked fresh garden earth is inviting.

...Or Just to Dig
Of course, some dogs just dig for fun, like kids in a sandbox. Puppies are especially prone to this kind of digging.

SOLUTION
Unfortunately, digging around the backyard, whether normal or not, can be destructive, unsightly, and annoying. It's also very hard to stop. It is useless and counterproductive to punish your dog for performing this natural activity. The best way to stop the objectionable behavior is to offer a palatable alternative. To prevent potentially destructive digging:

- **Keep your dog inside more.** The more he's inside, the less opportunity he'll have to dig outside. The comfort he'll get from being near you will reduce anxiety that may lead to digging.
- **Reduce his number of toys, especially edible ones.** Dogs tend to bury leftovers, not things for immediate consumption. If a dog has too many toys or bones, he will bury some of them to protect them. Dogs also tend to bury the toys that they like the least. If one toy keeps getting buried, your dog is trying to tell you something: Throw it away.
- **Make him his very own earthbox.** Bring along some of his favorite toys or treats, and play with your dog in the box. Praise and treat him for digging in the appropriate place. You might even show him the way by digging a bit in the sanctioned spot yourself.
- **Put up a dog-proof fence to protect your flowers and vegetables.** It will give your garden an air of sophistication and keep it completely secure from your digger as well.

On the other hand, you can let your dog find out for himself that digging is no fun. I have heard of

Digging can be a sign of boredom, loneliness, excessive heat, a desire to escape, or it can just be something your dog does for fun.

Keep tempting food or other items out of your dog's reach. If he can get to something he wants, he will take the opportunity.

people burying a hose in their dog's favorite digging spot, hiding in the house, and turning on the hose when the dog digs in that spot. In this case, the dog is not associating the soaking with you but as a negative consequence of the digging activity.

FOOD STEALING OR COUNTER CRUISING

Dogs are opportunists, and most of the time it's too much to expect your dog to ignore perfectly good food placed where he can easily get to it.

SOLUTION

This is a problem that is much easier to manage than to prevent; just assume that anything your dog can get at, he will. How can you manage the problem? By dog-proofing your house. Do not tempt your dog. Put the bread in the bread box, and don't let the chicken thaw on the counter. A dog is not able to resist available food, so put it out of his sight and mind.

JUMPING UP

Puppies often jump up to greet their owners. They are trying to lick your face, and that's the only way they can figure out how to get there. The problem is that while most of us don't mind a jumping puppy, the behavior gets less cute as the dog gets older—and bigger. You can change this behavior, even if your dog is an adult, but you'll have to be firm and consistent— meaning that you can't allow him to do it sometimes and then forbid it at other times.

SOLUTION

The key to solving this problem is first to anticipate when your dog is likely to jump. He is expecting you to respond in some way, so the key is not to respond—at all. Don't reward him with a look, a word, or a gesture. Never knee him in the chest, step on his toes, grab his paws, push him off, or touch him in any way. Simply cross your arms and walk away. If your dog is in the habit of jumping, he will not understand what's happening and at first will try harder and harder to get your attention. Be firm. Do not reward this behavior with a response.

Eventually, he will give up and sit down—or at least calm down—with all four feet on the floor. At that point, reward him immediately with a small treat or a good pet.

Practice giving him rewards when he's calm, never when he's excited. Once you solve the jumping problem, take it a step further and ask him to sit down upon your arrival. (For information on how to teach the sit, see Chapter 4.) Have a treat ready.

Also, remember that everyone in the house has to go along with this training program. If even one person rewards the dog for jumping up, the behavior will continue.

MOUTHING AND NIPPING

Mouthing and nipping are normal canine behaviors, especially for puppies, who have very sharp, needle-like teeth. Dogs learn about their universe through their mouths. They have no hands and are hungry all the time, so mouthing, chewing, and nibbling is simply a way to discover what's out there.

If you are lucky, your little puppy has learned what is called "bite inhibition," or the ability to control the force of his bite. This is a little trick puppies are supposed to learn from their littermates, who shriek and cry when bitten too hard in play. Some behaviorists theorize that puppy

Did You Know?

Puppies have 28 "milk teeth," which erupt between the third and sixth week of age. Adult dogs have 42 teeth, including molars that puppies initially lack.

teeth are actually as sharp as they are so that puppies will learn bite inhibition. If you're not lucky, or if you got your puppy at too young an age, he may not have learned this valuable skill yet. Unless you want to settle for being a pincushion for the rest of your life, it's your job to teach this skill to your dog.

SOLUTION

What you don't want to do when your dog nips you is yell at, shake, or hit your puppy. This will only succeed in frightening him. If your puppy nips you, cry "Ow!" in a high-pitched puppy voice. If he has your hand, try not to yank it away; that will make him try to hold it by biting down harder.

The trick is to get the dog to remove his mouth from your skin. If he removes his mouth immediately, you can continue to play with him by offering him a toy or other acceptable substitute for your hand. If that doesn't work, just yip sadly and walk away. Game over.

Don't make your absence long, however. Come back in a couple of minutes and try again. Puppies don't have a very good sense of time, and by coming back quickly, you'll have an opportunity to repeat the lesson.

Teaching Bite Inhibition

You can help your dog learn bite inhibition by hiding a treat in your hand. (If he's a hard nipper, you might want to wear gloves.) Close your fist over the treat, and allow him to nose gently for it. If he starts nipping, clench down harder. Don't open your hand and give him the treat until he takes it gently. Amazingly, he will soon learn to "soften his bite," but don't expect your puppy to develop bite inhibition instantaneously. It can easily take up to a week, even with steady work, but you will get there.

Another way to teach bite inhibition is by playing tug-of-war. While this game has received some bad press of late, dogs love it, and when you do it right, it is not only harmless but also a great training aid. It is especially good for puppies who lack confidence.

For a game of tug-of-war, use a long rope toy. Never tug on anything that brings your precious fingers too close to your dog's teeth. Play nicely, and make sure that you win the game most of the time. (The more timid

Quick Tip

If you have a puppy who tends to mouth or bite, avoid tugging games and other activities that may overstimulate him until he has mastered bite inhibition.

Dogs ordinarily learn bite inhibition as puppies by playing with others in their litter.

your puppy is, the more you can let him win.)

If yelping and stopping play doesn't work after a week, you may have to ratchet up the training. Purchase a head halter and attach a short leash to it. When your puppy bites too hard, pull gently on the leash, which will have the effect of closing his mouth. Say "Off" at the same time, and stop play. When your puppy calms down, you can resume play. If he still bites too hard, repeat the procedure.

COMMIT TO YOUR CANINE

Many of the behaviors described in this section are termed "phobic" or "obsessive." But they are really just adaptations to bad situations. Dogs are social animals, and studies show that dogs who develop obsessive or compulsive behaviors tend to be single dogs who are left on their own for a long time every day.

Dog behaviorists have noted again and again that the single most important aspect to controlling a dog problem is the commitment of the owner. In other words, owners who are not truly committed to keeping and caring for their dogs have more problems with them and are much less likely to try to solve their problem behaviors.

Boldfaced numbers indicate illustrations.

ACKNOWLEDGEMENT

Special thanks to Adam Taliercio and Stephanie Fornino for their editing, which is both expert and kind. It was also needed.

PHOTO CREDITS

ABOUT THE AUTHOR

Diane Morgan is an assistant professor of philosophy and religion at Wilson College, Chambersburg, PA. She has authored numerous books on canine care and nutrition and has also written many breed books, horse books, and books on Eastern philosophy and religion. She is an avid gardener (and writes about that, too). Diane lives in Williamsport, Maryland, with several dogs, two cats, some fish, and a couple of humans.